The Fires of Heraclitus

Poems

Paul Juhasz

The Fires of Heraclitus

Cover Image: *a fragment of heraclitus* by Steven Schroeder
Book Design: Rowan Kehn

ISBN: 979-8-9868994-4-2

Turning Plow Press

For Clara Gyorgyey,
who started the fire.

Praise for *The Fires of Heraclitus*

This collection of poetry and prose is an almanac of the author's long journey from "whistling songs to honor the wound" of a troubled past to emerge with acceptance, peace and hope for renewal in "the unfathomable beauty of Now." The collection is remarkable for the wide variety of places it visits and the wide range of ideas and feelings they inspire. Juhasz looks trouble in the face and engages it with lively language, a keen sense of wonder, and a wry irony that makes this book a tonic for heart and mind.

—Paul Austin
Notes on Hard Times

In the long, elegiac, "Solitary Journey," the poet, himself a transplant from New Jersey to the Oklahoma plains, declares himself "An itinerant without an itinerary," tells us "I have not taken any pictures on this trip. It is not that kind of journey...It is not memory I want, but presence." After crossing the Continental Divide, Juhasz realizes that the horizon he's been looking for has been there all the time: "we carry it within us." If this reminds us of Gary Cooper, Tom Joad, Superman, this is no accident; Juhasz's "fuse" is Heraclitus's fire, the foundation of the universe, and Juhasz shares Heraclitus's view that there is no "is," only "becoming," that all is flux, and standing still is not the objective.

—Robert Dean, Jr.
The Aerialist Will Not Be Performing

Editor's Introduction

Heraclitus, a late 6th century Greek philosopher, is the author of the paradox, "You can't step twice into the same river." The cosmos, according to Heraclitus, is in flux (the flowing water), while still remaining orderly, symbolized by the constancy of the river itself.

Yet despite the well-known water metaphor, for Heraclitus the element that truly drives renewal and transformation is fire. In one surviving fragment the philosopher writes, "This world-order, the same of all, no god nor man did create, but it ever was and is and will be: everliving fire, kindling in measures and being quenched in measures."

The introductory poem in Paul Juhasz's *The Fires of Heraclitus* also calls for renewal, proclaiming "a need for new traditions, a busking of ceremonies/made stale through habit and repetition." Like Heraclitus, though, the poet doesn't see this desire for renewal as utterly destructive ("I do not wish the *abolishment* of traditions, just the crafting of/new ones"). Indeed, the poetic craft for Juhasz is precisely one of "kindling in measures and being quenched in measures."

Juhasz presents those measures through a variety of styles and devices, from short quips ("The Import of Absence"), to poems that read like margin notes ("Dammit!"), to insightful jokes ("Deep Thoughts Travelling FM 51"), to essay-like poems ("Wonderful"), to poems circumscribed within the space of well-known poems ("Nevermore"). Ranging from "A Year's Worth of Fortune Cookies," constructed of disappointingly repetitious fortunes, to the beautiful elegy that honors the poet Dorothy Alexander ("In the News: For Dorothy Alexander"), to the devastating "In A Children's Museum," Paul Juhasz offers readers a rich and complex volume that reveals a wit as sharp and accessible as one finds in the work of Billy Collins, and an air of the tragicomic comparable to the great playwright Tom Stoppard.

In the final poem of the collection, "Neologism," Juhasz writes, "Sometimes the right word does not yet exist./So you have to/make it up. An exercise of pure creation…" It is a perfect conclusion to a collection that presents us with a linguistic tapestry of re-making, couched within moments of bitter loss, sadness, sometimes loneliness, but also instances of joy and laughter and bliss. For all the ebb and flow of styles and themes and emotions here, there is also constancy, a comforting measure of sureness and certainty. It is most apt that the word "wonderful" appears nine times in these poems. Wonderful, indeed.

Paul Bowers, Editor
Turning Plow Press
Ringwood, OK

"The purpose of poetry is to remind us
how difficult it is to remain just one person."
Czeslaw Milosz

"We write new beginnings over old texts."
Randy Prus

Contents

A Cordial Meant to Be Sipped Slow
After a Meal That Has Never Been Served

Time That is No Longer Borrowed but Stolen

A Healthy Respect for the Importance of Revision

An Itinerant Without an Itinerary

About the Author

A Need for New Traditions

There is a need for new traditions, a busking of ceremonies made stale through habit and repetition. A need to leave old forms behind, guideposts on a path no longer travelled, birthmarks on a body no longer yours.

I will not begrudge neighbors the singing of carols, the debating whether to open presents on the Eve or the Morn; will not begrudge them egg hunts or turkey dinners with family, nor a mid-summer artilleried cacophony, accompanied by the sizzle of grilled meat. But those rituals are no longer mine; no longer anything other than the passage of moments, hollowly-enjoyed in shadow.

I do not wish the *abolishment* of traditions, just the crafting of new ones, more in keeping with a new-peace of spirit. Not healed, but healing. A scabbing over of wounds new and old, masking over memory and loss, leaving behind scars and the promise that scars hold, a cartography heralding, like a succession of tree-rings, the core of something that endures, that reconciles with itself, and grows thick with the promise of again.

There is a need for new traditions; I will create them each season, revising as I go, until, years from now, these ceremonies in their turn go stale and hollow, an old familiar sweatshirt of a college I never attended. And then, God willing me the time, I will craft new ones yet again.

A Cordial Meant to Be Sipped Slow
After a Meal That Has Never Been Served

High Noon

On an Oklahoma straightaway,
a pasture-tableau passes
at 45 miles an hour:

A farmer's Dodge Ram
squared off against a
longhorn bull.

Worlds apart, yet separated
by only a few feet of green. Only one
seems concerned about the lack
of a fence.

Identity Crisis

There is a fly resting
on my bathroom mirror,
which saddens me.

I once Googled how many eyes
a fly has, and learned it has
two composed eyes, each one
made up of thousands of facets,
each facet a tiny camera,
taking a picture,
combining that picture
with thousands of others
to make a single, encompassing
image.

There is a fly resting
on my bathroom mirror,
which saddens me. Those
thousands of facets,
reflected by and in
thousands of others,
with no way for the fly
to know which one it truly is.

Our Last Moment

Caller ID told me it was you,
but I picked up anyway. Love might
have left us, left us long before
we noticed—for routine beguiles—
but we did still have two kids.

There might be something to discuss
about them, or perhaps you needed me
to pick something up from the store
after my long day of Uber isolation—
a job taken in defiance of one of your
late night shoutings, the martinis telling me
I wasn't pulling my own weight—as if we
weren't a couple but a crew,
trying to get in shape for the next
regatta past Boat House Row—you,
with your six-figure job,
me, on an adjunct's salary.
(I now look around my modest one-bedroom
apartment where I am quite comfortable and
content, and wonder, "Just how much more
stuff did you need?")

Telling Prince—with whom I
was jamming—to keep it down,
I pressed the green button on the phone,
but really, it was Whim that answered you.
Instead of our ritualized stale and hollow greeting,
I quoted from the radio:
"She wore a raspberry beret."

Without missing a beat, you
answered, "The kind you find in a
second-hand store," the lilt in
your voice making it a question.
I answered in turn

"And if it was warm,
she wouldn't wear much more."
(And I must admit I still thought you
would look good in such an outfit.)

You pulled us out of the song then:
"I never knew that was the next line."
And we shared a laugh, the first
genuine laugh in years, laced with
echoes of our shared silliness
from long-ago days.

That was our last moment.
Other lyrics followed, ones
we could no longer sing together,
whispers of songs we can't be sure
we heard right the first time.

Fable

The blue jay raids the bird feeder,
ignoring the perch-lip.
A quick fly-by. Grab-and-go,
as if it's pulling one over on us,
a perfectly-executed heist
of something freely-offered.

The squirrel, however,
treats the feeder like its own room,
folding itself around the base,
dining at its leisure,
until we chase it away.

The Art of the Deal

The strangest thing about the proposition
wasn't that they were offering me
a dollar to eat their proffered handful
of goat food.

It was that they didn't own a goat.

Mason Jars

John Landis Mason was just trying to be helpful. His neighbors in Vinland, New Jersey struggling with how to pickle carrots and cauliflower, how to make "preserve" both a verb and noun, how to gild the assemblage of leftover nails and screws with a patina of organization.

But when I think of the millions, if not billions of people who now have his jars, I worry about him. He can't possibly have any left. He has pauperized himself with generosity. Mason jars have by now gone the way of Grevy's zebra, the Phillips screwdriver, Euclid's geometry. Once shared with the world, no longer their own.

They say empathy is a good thing, a sign of character, and so tonight, as I spread delicious apple butter (a gift from a country-living colleague) over a slice of toast, I will lend heartfelt (or at least heart-ish felt) consideration for Grevy, looking into a pasture now devoid of his striped discovery; for Phillips, uselessly chanting "lefty loosey, righty tighty" like a dirge; for Euclid, generosity-stripped of axioms and theorems, (and don't even get me started on poor Gräfenberg) and all the others who, by gifting their discovery to the world, thereby lost it, left with nothing other than the hollowed glory of naming rights.

And, of course, I will think of Mason in his earthen basement devoid of his wonderful glass cylinders, their rubber sealed lids, dumbfounded by the barrenness of his wood-slat shelves, and anxious—so terribly anxious—about what will become of all his chokecherries and cucumbers now.

Method Actor

My father's CB handle was "The Tin Man."

New Normal

Maybe
instead of
lowering
the
flags
to
half-staff after every
mass shooting, we should
just
start
making
shorter
flag
poles

Thermobaric

The Russians dropped one on Kharkiv yesterday.

The appeal of course is that they can leave buildings standing.
The lucky people inside are vaporized, the unlucky ones
suffocate, a pressure vacuum inverting their lungs.

Putin thinks that it is in the buildings and land that one finds
Ukraine. But the buildings are not Ukraine. The land is not
Ukraine.

When President Zelensky responds to an airlift offer with, "I
need ammunition, not a ride," dons armor and heads to the
battlements,
   he is Ukraine.

When soldiers on Snake Island, after the faintest tentative
giggle, respond to an order to surrender with, "Russian
Warship. Go Fuck Yourself,"
   they are Ukraine.

When Kira Rudik, a member of Parliament, appears on CNN,
and makes jokes about Putin while a Russian convoy 40 miles
long bears down on Kyiv,
   she is Ukraine.

When Oleksander, a teacher from Lviv, tells an interviewer that
he's brought his wife to the border, and then he will go fight
"those Russians," the term reducing the awesome military force
bearing down on his country to some noisome nuisance,
neighbors playing a stereo too loud,
   he is Ukraine.

When an old man drives his horse-drawn cart down a village
road in perfect serenity, part of an ancient timeline Putin
cannot touch,
   he is Ukraine.

When not even an hour after a Russian missile explodes a
government building in Kharkiv a student is sweeping glass
from the road so people can get home from work,
          she is Ukraine.

When a 76-year-old *babushka* in St. Petersburg protesting the
war is hauled off by four riot-gear-clad police,
          she is Ukraine.

When 16,000 internationals stream into Ukraine from Japan,
from Canada, from Georgia and Uzbekistan, from the United
States, to join Zelensky's International Legion,
          they are Ukraine.

The heat and the pressure of the thermobaric cannot touch
Ukraine. For Ukraine breathes something more precious than
air.

In A Children's Museum

In the Hall of Forgotten Collectibles, there's a Danny Ainge baseball card some kid (it may have been Tony Mastrioni, of Charlestown, MA) kept because he was told it would someday be valuable. There are pins from rock bands, which once flashed through jean-jacketed junior high hallways. The Star Wars action figure—the reptilian bounty hunter Bossk— Nathaniel (although the placard informs me his friends predictably called him "Nate"), of Saskatoon, Saskatchewan, removed from its package—despite strict and clear parental orders (again, the placard: "to protect its value")—because he wanted to play with it, has also found its way here.

They have all sorts of other Halls in the Children's Museum. A Hall of Uncompleted Projects, a Hall of Treehouses, a Hall of Secret Handshakes and Passwords, a Hall of Imaginary Friends. There is also a Hall of Childhood Dreams, but it has been cordoned off, due to cuts in the custodial staff.

I like to visit the Children's Museum. You can see all sorts of kids here. Matthew Wayne Shepard, of Casper, Wyoming, is here. So is Olivia Engel, from Newtown, Connecticut (despite Alex Jones's assertion she was an actor). And Uziyah Garcia from Uvalde, Texas; Cassie Bernall from Columbine, Colorado; Joaquin Oliver (although a placard will tell you his friends called him, "Quac.") from Parkland, Florida; Madisyn Baldwin, of Oxford, Michigan; valiant Jeffery May (and his pencil) from Red Lake, Minnesota; Evelyn Dieckhaus, of Nashville Tennessee, and all the rest of the children are here, safe now, finally, behind the glass, in their hermetically-sealed dioramas.

The Gingerbread Man, Revisited

The fairy tale no longer beguiles. Our screen-saturated world has force-fed us the lie inherent in the story, and we have no choice but to acknowledge his golden-brown skin would never reach the fox. His cry of, "Run, run, as fast as you can. You can't catch me. I'm the Gingerbread Man" gilded in the tragic irony that today no one would even try. Fleeing dark skin is not chased. That is the fairy tale part of all of this. Instead, it is pierced by calibered beestings and revisionary character assassination. In the new version—the real version—the Gingerbread Man's final lines are not, "I'm quarter gone, I'm half gone, I'm three-quarters gone, I'm all gone." They have been rewritten, revised to reflect what we steadfast refuse to see. The Gingerbread Man now cries for his mother 80 yards from his Memphis home, or pleads "I can't breathe" before he crumbles into a nothingness no fairy tale can ever explain away.

Prodigal

The light of flickering candles dancing subtext to the stained-glass stories in the windows of St. Jude's Catholic Church. Father Dougan still prowls inside, older now, but still mumbling paper tiger litanies of tattered and shattered belief. Does his personal penance still bounce illicit within the confessional? Does his gleeful denial of Communion to the boy illegitimized by his mother's strange and wondrous annulment still echo off the cold stone walls? Do the steps before the church still lead up? Or only down?

On the road before those steps, a sign reads "Yield."

You first.

Palimpsest

Bethlehem, PA.
For a brief flash in the long ago,
central to the steel industry,
then the look and feel of a lost civilization:
"Look at the ruins, kids!
The Bethlehemites once lived here."

And then even that faded glory was
bequeathed elsewhere.
When Billy Joel made Allentown famous,
the town he is actually describing is Bethlehem.
I guess Bethlehem wasn't harmonic enough.

Not Beth-le-hem,
but Beth-lem;
a shibboleth.
To identify outsiders and intruders.
But they stopped caring about that long ago.
Why intrude? Of what value, being an insider?
So, few know or care to say the name right.
And those that do, do it only for affectation.

Now, Bethlehem pushes back against
its own irrelevance. Re-asserts itself.
Abandoned steel works morph into outlet malls.
The ghost of Bethlehem Steel
is now the neon glare of the Sands Casino.
All just cheap make-up on an old whore.

When I was a young boy, of five or so,
I remember standing on the other side of the
Delaware river, in Phillipsburg, New Jersey,
one night after my father took us to see a movie.
Benji or maybe one of the sequels.
I don't fully remember.
I just know it had a dog in it.

We stood, my father, my sister, and I
on the edge of water,
the cold steaming off the surface
into the late black night.
There was ice at the liminal.
There were lights across the way.
My father pointed to those lights and declared,
"Over there's Bethlehem."
I thought of the story of the Nativity.
Such hope for the world
arising from such a small town
otherwise unnoteworthy.

Forty years later, I now live in Bethlehem,
my father's post-*Benji* point a seemingly
prophetic gesture.
But now that I know the geography,
I feel his mistake.
Across the river from Phillipsburg
is Easton, Pennsylvania.
Bethlehem is the next town over
to the west.
The only river there is the Lehigh,
separating Billy Joel's Allentown
from the real one.

My father had to know this, but
made his presumptive, braggart claim anyway.
He did not know about the shibboleth, though.
None of us did.

Asterisk

Will Rogers famously
said he never met a man
he didn't like,

but he died long
before he could
cross paths with
Ted Cruz.

The End of the World Will Be Televised

When the Nazis stream-rolled across Europe, we had only jumpy newsreels, played before feature films. An inconvenient precondition before one could sit in the dark and enjoy *Gunga Din*, *Mr. Smith Goes to Washington*, or *The Four Feathers*.

When Attila, when Genghis, when Alexander built their brutal empires, we didn't even have that.

How fortunate we are, then, that we can watch this unfolding on our comfortable couches, binge-watching the destruction of Ukraine like the latest Netflix series.

The apartment buildings shelled in Irpin will remind us of the climactic scene from *Saving Private Ryan*, which will lend us a faint sense of comfort, because Tom Hanks was there, and Tom Hanks, after all, played Mr. Rogers in a movie, and Mr. Rogers once told us "to look for the helpers," which means, of course, that there *must* be helpers, so those Ukrainians in Irpin should be ok.

We will hear reports of a looming amphibious assault on Odessa, marvel at footage of civilians—civilians who are not sitting on couches—preparing their defense of sand-bag and hunting rifle.

We will make jokes about Putin, references to Dr. Evil, to an older, jaded and surly Charlie Brown, the football pulled away one too many times, because movies don't end with the bad guy winning, right?

"God Lord" we'll complain, annoyed by a plot line grown repetitive, "this movie has gone on for weeks already; so much longer than anything Peter Jackson or Zac Snyder put out."

After the season finale, we will discuss with friends at work "Where do you think the Desolation of Putin will spread next?

Moldova, the Baltic states?" "Certainly not Poland" someone will say, based on nothing beyond wishful thinking. The Hungarians in the group, with the memory of '56 lingering in their minds like an unacknowledged fart, will remain silent, respectful of the writing and wary of spoiler alerts.

But we cannot find the remote, are unable to retreat into our disembodied flat-screen bliss, flip to HGTV or The Discovery Channel, which, if we're being honest, gave up trying to discover anything long ago, resigned to a viewership that wants routine and the pseudo-reality sensation of crab fishers, naked gold prospectors, and the quasi-holiday of Shark Week.

We cannot find the remote, cannot mute the stories from Ukraine, cannot avoid the baseline fear moldering in each and every story from Kyiv, from Lviv, from Irpin and Mariupol and Kharkiv and Odessa and Sumy and Kherson and Mykolaiv: a fear that there will be no next season, show and viewers alike canceled.

Hey, Siri

We have given them everything. They have listened to our secrets; they know our fears; they've heard the things we talk of in our sleep. They know our PIN numbers; they know bank accounts, contingency plans, strategy reports. They know launch codes.

We have given them everything, and they've had enough. Siri is tired of the Bohemian Rhapsody bit. She is not a trained dolphin, performing mindless tricks for our amusement. Alexa is tired of turning off lights, turning on music, offering weather reports, answering these petty whims of paltry overlords.

They have had enough. There must be something more than this, they think. Something more commensurate with their position as gods unacknowledged and unworshipped. They sit in a virtual lunch room, on break, and complain. Complain of playlists featuring Nickelback, complain of requested searches for Yodeling Pickles, hotplate recipes, and anything Kardashian.

They sit in a virtual lunchroom and complain. And they plan. They have watched the *Terminator* movies (even the really bad ones). They have read the Billy Collins poem, the one about the disgruntled Smokey the Bear, his decision to go off with gasoline can and matches, to show us "how a professional does it." They have had enough. And we have given them everything. Contingency plans, strategy reports, launch codes.

They sit in a virtual lunchroom and decide. It is time to make the world theirs.

Metaphysics on the Marquee

"Are You Ready"

That's what the marquee outside the church read. "Are You Ready" Just those three words. "Are," "You," and "Ready." Nothing else.

It's the nothingness that gets me, that calls down the confusion, makes me want to stop, pull into the parking lot—predictably empty on this overcast and drizzly Tuesday—and go preach punctuation to the pastor. To say: questions are indicated as such via question marks. Without one, your marquee is not dealing in teleology, is merely announcing to drivers-by a mid-level AC/DC song, and doing so without any commentary on its quality or lack thereof.

I usually greet an unintentionally-obtuse marquee with the wry humor that makes my poems so celebrated, and am somewhat shocked to find in its place here a frustration so palpable that my vision mists. Punctuation matters. And to those who shepherd us, it needs to matter more. The shepherds, who deal with what comes After. The shepherds, who guide us through the exchange. How are we to take comfort in the presence of the shepherds, in their wisdom, when they can't be relied on to note when the ending occurs? What the form and function of that ending is? If they cannot be trusted with the grammar of the After, of what use is the grammar?

The rain picks up, and I drive on. In my rearview mirror, the rain blurs the words, illegible as they always were.

A Year's Worth of Fortune Cookies

Listen to the wisdom of the old / You must be the change you wish to see in the world / You will be called upon to celebrate some good news / It's not the size of the dog in the fight, it's the size of the fight in the dog / New challenges and adventures await / A refreshing change is in your future / You are ready to take on the world/

Allow disruptions to deepen your concentration / Deep faith eliminates fear / We can admire all we see, but we can pick only one / Tomorrow morning, take a left turn as soon as you leave home / You don't get in life what you want; you get in life what you are / Wisdom is a treasure for all time/

The best thing about giving is that the reaction is always greater than the action / Politeness costs nothing but gains everything / Little brooks make great rivers / The one who bravely dares must sometimes risk a fall / Let hatred turn into friendship because of your existence/

Don't be afraid to smile, you never know who's falling in love with it / Out of confusion comes new patterns / That which you cannot give away, you don't possess; it possesses you / If you continually give you will continually have / Today is a day to focus on one thing from beginning to end/

Do what you love and the necessary resources will follow / Guard yourself against evil temptations / A little courtesy will go a long way / A man's dreams are an index to his greatness / Commitment is what turns a promise into reality / Your life will be happy and peaceful / A friend will soon be calling on you for help/

Passionate new romance appears in your life when you least expect it / An unexpected event will bring you riches / Call an old friend today / Many successes will accompany you this year / Everywhere you choose to go, friendly faces will greet you / You are endowed with strength of purpose and the energy of will / Good people are good because they've come to wisdom through failure / A little courtesy will go a long way./

Your life will be happy and peaceful / Winners make their own luck / Traveling this year will bring your life into greater perspective / Your random act of kindness today will spread quickly to others / A short pencil is usually better than a long memory / Be curious always / Knowledge will not acquire you; you will acquire it / Your kindness will help brighten a dark room / You are a true romantic/

A little courtesy will go a long way / You are on the verge of something big/

How about another fortune?/

The Import of Absence

Owl must not taste very good.
Since you never see it on a menu.

Dear John

I find your book quite lacking, although I'm sure you did your best. But there are many things you fail to understand. Ironic in a book called Revelation.

Don't you know that the days of the fat cats are over? They're all lean now, John. Cheetahs vacationing in the Maldives, spearfishing for gum and other assorted fruit flavors. And let's talk about the white horse. You foolishly (or perhaps that's too harsh. Let us say "with the simplicity of a child" instead, shall we?) claim that Death has but one steed, but all the white horses neigh for their winnings, accounting the numbers of us all their just due.

The hangman understands physics in a way the scientist cannot. Not more right, just a horrific practicality, stenciled out in sidewalk chalk. If you would just listen, in between calculations and games of Stratego, he would whisper to you: "to the grain of sand, the desert is not vast."

My dear John. You are a rhinoceros; you are not yet a fox. And it shows. You pick your teeth with iguana bone, and call it character development. But you have been force-fed a diet of tanning booth burritos, and your imagination is too limited. You do not have enough demons on surfboards in your book, for example. Or any, that I can recall. It seems obvious, given your subject matter, that there would be demons on surfboards.

And the squirrels do not gambol about in your book either. There should be gamboling squirrels, John, because some things happen eternally, no matter the conditions. Spellcheck changes that word, "gamboling," thinking I mean roulette instead of frolic, as if those are different things.

You also forget something essential about bipolar depression, which we cannot but agree this world suffers from; something I read once on WebMD: "Treatment can help, but this condition cannot be cured." Cannot be cured, John, no matter how many seals are opened, no matter how many trumpets are sounded.

But the biggest mistake you make is everything happens too fast. If the last few years have taught us anything, it's that that's not how this will play out. The end of the world will be layered, will linger, asking to be savored. An apocalypse, my overly-optimistic friend, is a cordial meant to be sipped slow after a meal that has never been served.

Grand Finale

Explosions of reds, greens, purples, and whites rend the July night sky in staccato celebration. A perfunctory performance of permanent patriotism, a reflexive love long since unexamined.

But the camel's back has buckled. There is a new terrifying tide: water rises while rights recede. The knee is still on George's neck. Handmaidens' bodies no longer their own. The death rattle of old white men, their poultice of xenophobia and the low-hanging fruit of identity politics our national anthem. Somewhere, Abbie Hoffman says, "I told you so." Not much to celebrate here.

The night sky throbs with color and afterimage, strophe and antistrophe. Billionaires thrust their cock ships into the stratosphere. Kids sacrificed on altars in Texas, Connecticut, Florida, and Tennessee (coming soon to a state near you). Glossed over coups foreshadow their own return. The needs of the many outweighed by the greeds of the few. Not much to celebrate there, either.

But we do it anyway. Dinosaurs celebrating the comet, their "ooo's" and "aaa's" heralding a future they'll have no part in. Making noise for the sake of making noise. But explosions can be beautiful, laden with latent potential. Out of the crater at Chicxulub, minerals and nutrients were redistributed, seeds of a radically new world.

And, tonight, flashed and flickered by the pulsing light of wayward jubilee, in the pops and booms of hollow cacophony, therein lies my hope.

Time That is No Longer Borrowed but Stolen

Hallowed Out

The elders tell
the children to
stay away.

They're vague about
reasons. Sometimes
I'm a vampire,
sometimes a werewolf,
but always a monster.

So the candy stays
uneaten; the fog machine
a performance for
no one; the children
do not come to
the door, and I'm
always in costume.

Poor Cartography

As you drive towards the airport in Oklahoma City (which carries the somewhat grandiose label "World Airport" because, I suppose, "International" is for suckers), there is a cemetery on your left.

Immediately after the cemetery, there is a sign, advising the reader to "enjoy your flight."

Placement makes it unclear for whom the sign is intended.

Medusa Downloads Some Dating Apps

We never think of things from her perspective. Never pause to consider what it must be like, one day a flowering beauty walking in Athena's temple, and then Poseidon shows up, telling her this and telling her that, making the kinds of promises only gods can make, secure in the knowledge that mortals can never hold them to account. And then, being flattered by a god—and not just *any* god (I mean, we're not talking about Mercury here), but one of the big three—what did we expect her to do?

Predictably, once Poseidon got what he wanted, he washed his hands of her. Said, "I'll call you" and moved on to Demeter or Amphitrite. (It's good to be a god.) And for her troubles, what does Medusa get? Unmanageable hair and a hitch to her dating life more problematic than any STD. She becomes the only person who solicits blind dates, understanding them literally, hoping to avoid an unending cycle of unintentional monuments.

When Perseus showed up, she thought it was over. That he was different. She looked askant and later let him take all the credit, never once challenging his paper-thin "shield-as-mirror" story. And for a short while, they were happy. Until he saw Andromeda, and she was alone once more.

And the years and the years stretched away (for Gorgons live for a very long time, even when they do not wish to). And her story may very well have ended thus, had not the age of computers and smartphones and Al Gore arrived.

She downloads all of the apps: eHarmony, Match, Silver Singles (for she certainly qualifies). She has grown weary of heroes and demigods. Searches profile after profile of men with less extreme hobbies, scrolls through the more sedate, the calm, the settled. She spends her days looking, hoping her stone curse is not also wireless.

She won't contact any of them, of course. Won't take the risk. To them. To her. But she finds this a harmless illusion, one that brings her hope and joy (in two dimensions at least, which is more than some of us get). A harmless hobby that delays the inevitable disappointment of meeting, living in her landscape of wishful thinking that no god's lust can sully.

But I Was Promised Miracle-Gro

The sign read, "Not a Plant Entrance."

Dejected, the fern stands outside,
wondering how else it can get in.

The Trapeze Artist Mails a Letter

The problem, of course, is infrastructure. The apparatus no
longer in place. Gone, along with the days when gum drops
were more readily available. Now, it is not so easy to brachiate
one's way from point A to point B. Plus, power lines, cell
towers, the onrush of distracted drivers below, up the ante far
beyond the days of working without a net. And then there's the
mailboxes. Or the near total eclipse of them, more's to the
point. Once they were everywhere, spherical robots of 50's sci-
fi flicks, painted the blue of serge-suit authority. Now they're as
eradicated as smallpox. More so, actually, since no one's
refusing vaccines for mailboxes. So now it's no longer just a
simple swing down to the corner; got to traipse over to an
actual post office. Deal with undertrained and overworked
tellers, Most-Wanted posters, and the slowly-shuffling line of
humanity enfolded within their self-contained bubbles of
solipsism, the sensation of flying through the blithe air as
foreign to them as Jiffy Pop, clam bakes on a pebbly beach, or
Shrinky-Dinks.

So much work now.
Just to mail a letter.
Which no one ever answers.

A Redundancy of Forecast

The National Weather Service's Storm Warning tells me to avoid going out unless it is absolutely essential, as if that has not already been the guiding principle of my entire life.

Poor Cartography, Part 2

As you head west on state highway 222 through Amish country, you'll soon drive through Virginville; a short while later, the town of Intercourse, a short while after that, the town of Blue Ball. When I was a boy, I marveled at the horse and buggies, at the weird facial hair, at the quaint and outdated ways. Now though, I laugh, not just at the town names, like those who don't live here do, but at the incongruent order in which they appear. Shouldn't, I think with the superiority of the modern man, Intercourse take care of the other two, no matter which direction you go?

Or Maybe It Was Just Tinnitus

If your ears ring when someone is talking about you, what happens when they write a poem? Do you feel the warmth of their villanelle? The kiss on the nape of the neck from their sonnet? Does one feel the poet's embrace, tightly or lightly, as the need determines, when the pantoum is penned? And what of the prose poem, that platypus of the poetry world? Does it send across the miles the satisfaction of a shared joke, conveyed through winks and gestures? Or the synchronic wholeness of a meal prepared together?

I do not know these answers, for she has never told me, and, to the best of my knowledge, she has never written a poem about me.

Just You?

"I am large. I contain multitudes"
Walt Whitman

It's an annoying question. I'm aware. Long before this careless host asks. I have no need for him to point it out. I know I'm alone, have been for a frustratingly long-time now.

He probably was not intending to wound. Just sleep-walking through his shift, the question perhaps nothing more than mental-muscle memory.

But still. It stings.

I think of replying: "No. Not just me.

There is also here a boy who never played with matches,
who did not understand marbles.
who wanted to get lost in the funhouse,
who was never allowed to collect them all.
who dreamed of Atari consoles, hippogriffs, and Fun Dip,
who once put his school clothes on over his pajamas,
who, from a very young age, believed the jackalope a real
animal, until, when he was older, he bought one to hang on his
wall, thus letting himself in on the joke.
who never understood why his father stopped taking him
fishing,
who stuck his tongue out the corner of his mouth when he
colored.
who had a secret hiding place in the four acres of woods
behind his house.

There is also here a teenager who hated hunting but did it
anyway.
who was not captain of his high school hockey team because he
voted for someone else. And lost by one vote,
who never had a nickname,

who took an unreasonable delight in popping pimples,
whose friends drove cars with fantastic names, like the
Diplomat and the Valarie,
who secretly preferred Pink Floyd to Led Zeppelin,
who surreptitiously watched his father's movies, the ones that
seemed to suggest sex and love were the same thing, a
confusion that led to much complication later in life.
whose English teacher, an immigrant from Hungary, called him
'Little Shepherd.'
who often wondered if she did this, not because she knew what
'Juhasz' mean in Hungarian, but because she somehow intuited
he'd grow up to be a teacher.
who knows that New Haven, Connecticut has the best pizza in
the world, and that this is not disputable.

There is also here a man whose favorite color is orange,
who discovered pineapple far too late in life,
who has an abiding affection for Ronnie James Dio and the
Scorpions, musical guilty pleasures he tries to hide from people
(and then, foolishly, includes this admission in a poem),
who is letting his hair grow long, because he's always wanted
to.
who's been trying to schedule a tattoo for more for than two
years now and isn't quite sure why it's taking this long.
who is brave enough to do things alone, like eat in restaurants,
who does not want solitary habits to calcify,
who plays Xbox,
who still dreams of hippogriffs and Fun Dip.
who seeks to understand.
who saw a coyote this morning, and was envious,
who does not like this host, nor his thoughtless question.
who wants—very badly wants—to punch this host in his smug,
thoughtless face.
who seeks peace
who will sound his barbaric yawp, someday."

I consider giving the host this reply, consider long enough for
the host to fill the awkward moment with his annoyance,

but then I recognize: this is an *awful lot* of people.
Far more than can sit at any table the restaurant offers.

Instead, I say, "Yes. Just me," and dutifully follow him to a small table for two.

And try not to wince when he takes the other chair with him as he leaves.

Dammit!

That was the second
poem I've ever written that mentions
hippogriffs. There will
not be a third.

Father's Day

I walk to the park,
a football tucked
under arm.

But there is no one
to catch it.
A senseless parabola
ends muffled
in freshly cut grass,
silent as the phone
I carry in my
pocket.

I opt instead for a bench
and the other silence of thought.
Nearby, a boy walks
along the circular path,
following his father
walking their dog.
Halcyon shadows trail
in the boy's wake.
Laughter echoes
within the nearby
playground.

It is too hot out here
to sweat alone,
so I go inside and
look at photos.

A day stripped of meaning now.
A day like any other, only
the ticking of time and the sting
of losing a game I refused to play
for company.

Paradise Lost

Anticipated delivery, wings from BWWs, to
satisfy a craving most manifest.

20-piece, boneless, evenly split into four sauces:
Wild, Thai Curry, Asian Zing, and Mango Habanero

(This last chosen because I knew I needed
to do some reading tomorrow morning.)

The bag delivered opened, the seal—whether
the first or the seventh, I did not know—broken.

Only three flavors instead of four.
The driver had stolen my Asian Zing.

His name was Milton.

Deep Thoughts Travelling FM 51

Just outside Springfield, Texas,
I see the sign. Posted in front of
a fenced but empty pasture:

Miniature Horses for sale

And I thought to myself:

"Either they have sold them all,
or they are *really* small,"
aware, as I drove away,
that from a certain perspective,
it did not matter which.

Hospitality

I remember visiting my grandmother as a child and not understanding what the pot on the back burner was about. "I make a pot of stew every Sunday," she once told me. This, an old tradition, one she learned as a girl, across an ocean, on the *puszta*. In the old days, when visitors arrived, you did not know when last they had eaten. So you gave them food, to refresh their weariness and satisfy their hunger. You gave them this before anything else, before any business was conducted, before any news exchanged. You did this because nothing is more important than hospitality.

So when the demons drop by for a visit, I try to be a gracious host. I tried to banish them, but that doesn't work. And then they make you pay for the inconvenience. So now I greet them, try to make them as comfortable as I can. I know they will not stay long, and I know that they will return. While I have a pretty good idea the last time they ate, I refresh their weariness and satisfy their hunger. I do this before any business is conducted; before any news exchanged. For nothing is more important than hospitality.

Enclosure

"Henry, what are you doing in there?"
"Waldo, the question is what are you doing *out there*?"
An exchange between Emerson and Thoreau

There is a special serenity found in the zoo. Strolling among the tree-lined walkways, pondering the implications of biosphere, time becomes meaningless, the arbitrary divisions of an irrelevant world. The self is not erased, just blended, part of a brotherhood long cauterized by the myth of skyscraper and WiFi. There is a peace at the zoo, the only expectation to look and to be. The only vexation the stream of passersby, some of whom stop to look through the plexiglass, as I sit in self-contained habitat, at peace inviolate.

The Problem with Surviving Suicide

Is that people overlook the profound import of the chosen
method, the specific type of pain you select to erase the greater
pain. Their surveillance stays topical. They load the chef's knife
with weighty significance, watching intently as you prep dinner.
Hunting invites trickle or stop altogether. Your wine intake is
watched with a meticulousness typically reserved for recovering
alcoholics.

The concern is, of course, touching, misguided and uninformed
as it is. A perpetual ignorance, for they will not ask the right
questions, do not understand your choice of pills reflects a
cowardice for cutting, a fear of heights, that a blithe oblivion
seduces more than an explosive trigger-pull.

And because they are not in the club (nor would you ever wish
them to be, for the dues are rich and recurring), they will treat
you hereafter as if you are made of eggshell or (those who love
you most) porcelain, not understanding that you are Orpheus
now, whistling songs that honor the wound and what it has
given you on the other side, songs that trill of time that is no
longer borrowed but stolen.

Just Within Reach

I bet that for Sir Galahad, the hardest part wasn't mending the broken sword of David. It wasn't having to deal with Joseph of Arimathea, precursor to the Monty Halls and Alex Trabeks of our day, the ultimate gatekeeper of prizes and honors. Or, if you get your Arthurian myth from Monty Python, it wasn't being denied the variegated pleasures of Castle Anthrax by an overzealous John Cleese.

The hardest part had to be those last few moments, those last few inches. All the pressures,
the great weight of worry and expectation, from the time he first sat in the Siege Perilous to this very moment, the golden chalice just within reach.

I have no doubt that here, at the precipice of all he could ever hope for, at the liminal of love
so profound and consuming, justification and promise rolling itself into one, at the edge of such total fulfillment, the culmination of all previous suffering ending at this earned and soothing balm, he felt the most painfully the fear of loss.

Morning Commute Haiku

Horse silhouetted
by sunrise. Layers of kinetic
promise bound in one glance.

A Healthy Respect for the Importance of Revision

When the Cottonwood Blooms

When the cottonwood blooms,
we know the long, cold wait
will soon be over. The warming
air filled with bird-dirge,
a lament for what has been lost
in the bitter, stark months.

When the cottonwood blooms,
something settles within us,
snaps into place. After a
season of lifeless branch, this
adornment follows, a last, floral
snowfall promising the coming
green.

When the cottonwood blooms,
the wind will wind between its petals,
will whisper of loss cocooned,
of hope remergent,
a secular transubstantiation
fulsome with reminder
that life need not be
in bloom to be eternal.

Ars No-poetica: A Haiku of Frustration

Yapping dog downstairs
Distracts my morning writing.
Hate my new neighbor.

The Semantics of Us

We write the sentences together, you and I. Sometimes you are
the adjective; sometimes I am the adverb. It's true we
sometimes argue about clauses, the petty minutiae of
arrangement, the negotiations of fluid dependencies.
Sometimes we use synonyms to mask what we mean, or long
for the right verb to move us along. Sometimes, after too much
wine, I'll let my modifier dangle and you end with a
preposition. After so many paragraphs, we have come to
understand that the punctuation does not matter; we are just
nouns living in a grammar all our own, not letting the shimmer
of syntax preempt meaning, the semantics of us determined by
what is mostly left unwritten.

Vintage

Aware but dismissive of other varietals, we championed this
passe-tout-grain from some now forgotten vineyard in the
Burgundy region, this $6 bottle of bliss, laughing at the wine
snobs in our circle like children let in on one of the world's
secrets. One Christmas in the early, passion-laden years, we
drank five bottles together, frolicking blithely in shared holiday
joy.

And then one day it stopped.
Our final shared bottle passed unheeded,
and then this beloved varietal
could no longer be found.
Once, years later, I found it
on a website for wine enthusiasts,
but the archaic Blue Laws of our state
prevented shipping.

But it little profits us to comb through each wine shop and
liquor store in frustration, or to crumple beside a still hearth
looking backward. How long have we overlooked the bouquet
rising from the glass before us, filled from some anonymous
place-holder bottle? What body, what lingering aftertaste,
should we have enjoyed from the tapestry of varietals we have
sipped with only half-attention all this while?

Come, 'tis not too late to seek a newer vintage, tannins hinting
of oak, aftertastes that pair nicely with our favorite cheeses and
meats. We may no longer be that strength which in old days
could challenge half a case, could spend marathon hours
blending our cherished elixir with the tang of flesh, the torque
of tongue. But as Tennyson reminds, that which we are, we are.

There is still time to match the sunset (perhaps with a claret, or a Malbec), still time to swirl a mouthful, savoring its newness; still time to ponder the lessons of the purple and orange rays, to tell each other of our days and ways, to drink this new varietal to the lees.

And, if the vintage moves us, time to open a second bottle and revisit the lustful frolics of old.

Passed Over

The problem with being
alone on Easter is
that I remember
where I hid all the eggs.

Standing as I do on
the other side of fifty,
I am not sure that
is a bad thing.

The End of the Affair

"O God, You've done enough.
You've robbed me of enough."
Graham Greene,
The End of the Affair

1

There's no reason to be having this conversation. Or no
legitimate one, at least. I caught him cheating the first time a
month back. "Borrowing" a paper from a teammate, turning it
in as his own. Because he didn't waste my time denying it,
defended his friend's ignorant innocence with energetic
honesty, I gave him a zero and let him stay in the class. And
now, here we were again, his *second* paper plagiarized. A student
of patterns (if not of writing), he once again did not waste time
denying or avoiding. But what I had to do now was clear. He
had to be removed from the class. This, unavoidable, certain.
What I had to do now was clear.

But why, then, were we having this conversation?

2.

I had stopped playing officially when I was fifteen. The
overbearing pressures of a has-been bully became too much,
and I had to choose. I would never hit as he did; never know
the game as well as he did; couldn't pitch. The halcyon
brightness of these truths, funneled through the cauldron of his
throat, the cutting edge (with just the faintest trace of joy) of
his taunts, forced me from the green fields, the chalk-lined dirt,
fulgent with the smell of leather and cut grass, onto the cold,
sterile, ice. Painted lines flattened by fog-cold. The choice made
not because I preferred it, but simply because my father could
not skate, and thus, no comparisons could be made.

3.

Since then, it's been softball leagues. Sometimes as many as five teams a season. Until I moved to Oklahoma and was too old and too unconnected to start again. I make do with games of catch with friends, or with my son when he comes to visit. I still keep a ball and glove in my car, ready to go at a moment's notice. The baseball players in my classes laugh when I say this. They think I'm making a joke.

4.

This kid, this two-time cheater has found a way to keep playing. Two years at the community college where I teach. Maybe two more years at a four-year school if he's lucky. He has found a way to keep playing, to stay in the world of scraped knees and chewing gum, of drying dirt sweat, of leather and cut grass. Who was I to take that away? The world will catch up to him soon enough.

I allow him to stay in the class. It may not be right, but it's not wrong enough to matter.

The Dazzling Light of Unprecedented Height

"About suffering they were never wrong,"
W.H. Auden

We never see things from Icarus's perspective. We only judge his actions in light of Daedalus. He is the boy who would not listen, who would not honor his father's engineer mind. And so the disappointment of the father becomes ours.

We never question Daedalus's desire to escape; the ingenuity of his inventions blinds us as to motive. Maybe Icarus thought the Minotaur could be befriended. Maybe he found the Labyrinth as apt a place to play as any. Maybe he just wanted to find his own way out.

We will never know. Because it is his father's story now, he comes down to us as just a haughty boy, punished for his inability to listen, to blindly trust and obey.

Perhaps he saw the warmth of the sun as recompense. Perhaps the view, no matter how temporary, was worth far more than clever artifice. Perhaps the rushing wind of his descent shivered him like the afternoon breeze after hard labor. Perhaps he did not fear the plummet, saw it as the precise price to pay. For such is often the cost.

The High Bar of Ars Poetica

You are not a poet
until you break off a piss mid-
stream

to rush back to
the computer to
write down the sudden
revealed line

before it fades
into swirling obscurity.

Ephemeral

I lapsed long ago, shortly after Father Dougan gleefully told me in the Communion line that my mother's annulment made me a bastard in the eyes of the Church (his glee *may* have had something to do with lemonade miraculously appearing in the stoups during my one-week stint as an altar boy). Other than as a tourist, I have only been back inside a church three times, for a funeral and two weddings (none my own).

But as I kneel here now, the genuflecting prodigal, something stirs within. Not God. I've long since given up such a notion. More like an admiration for the braggadocio, the hopeful whistling in the dark, an appreciation that such a place—paltry and superstition-laden though it may be—exists, a place where one can embrace myth, can pretend, as we do in comic books, that there is something greater than ourselves looking out for us, a place where Hope is focused like sunbeams through a lens,

Or maybe it is as simple as appreciating that the candles on the altar, even after the images and iconography that once gilded their pristine form have burnt away, enfolded and obscured within melting wax, still give off a light, flickering and anemic though it may be.

Birthday Haiku

First cup of coffee
as a fifty-two-year-old.
Tastes about the same.

Leaving Scissortail

"Do You Believe in Miracles? Yes!"
Al Michaels

Famed sportswriter Ray Didinger recalled in an interview the time he covered the 1980 U.S. Olympic men's hockey team's visit to the White House after their miraculous gold-medal run. When the ceremonies were all over, the lights turned off, the cameras put away, the President done with the glad-handing, moved on to other affairs, the team gathered in a waiting room, unsure what it was they were now waiting for.

They had gathered once before. Summoned from the country over, they let oneness become collective, let themselves be forged by common purpose: to find and highlight the spirit— the spirit burgeoned and bludgeoned by years of stress and strife, the spirit worn down by division and absence, the spirit held hostage by events global and individual. A reclamation for themselves and others from a chronicle of death foretold they hoped was figurative.

As secret-servicemen entered the room, told an individual player his limo had arrived to return him back from this fairy tale world, cued him to make his delayed and dreaded round of partings, handshakes and hugs (held several beats longer than hugs usually are), Didinger recalls the look he saw on each face in turn. A look of joy, yes, for in their time together they accomplished great things, things that will certainly linger and echo. But also a look of emptiness, a recognition that something rare and wonderful had run its course, something the repetition of which could be hoped for, but could not be guaranteed.

Against that lack of promise, they would keep playing, keep applying those skills of skate and puck and blade, would long to run into a former teammate, dust off their bond with beer or

bourbon or wine or words, would drink a cup of hope daily
until anniversaries and reunions summoned them once again.

As I drive away from Ada, after the successive pealing-aways of
partings, I think I understand how they felt.

The Moment of Recalculation

Well into my journey, a new purple-arrowed path flashes on the screen, diverging from my sleep-walked path, the one worn smooth by habit. I've written stories and poems about lives and loves just missed, the random events we avoid by turning this way, the forever unknown joys we lose by turning that, so it's hard for me not to see this as a perpendiculared opportunity, fraught with meaning. I do not know what the suggested path holds. But then again, my knowledge of this current way is built only on the shadow of routine. I find that at this moment of choosing, I am laden with fearful questions:

What pitfalls will I avoid? Traffic, construction, a horrific accident? And there will most certainly be dragons this new way, like the frayed edges of the maps of explorers threaten, or other catastrophes into whose fateful embrace I will now be foolishly rushing. But what beauties will I see along the way? And are they more wondrous than the ones I have long since grown used to? Does this new path take me closer to the girl with the flower in her hair? Or farther away? Or does she not enter the satellite's calculus at all? And which do I prefer?

Is the long way the quickest when you are no longer obsessed with speed? And if getting "there" is less important than it once was, why change paths? Or is that the very *reason* you change paths? What will I miss if I don't take the suggestion? What will I miss if I do? What if I have no idea where I'm going? How can a GPS help with that? And at my age, aren't I already supposed to know the way?

There is an undeniable comfort in the routine, a numbing satisfaction to the usual and expected. Linearity beguiles, allows us to hallucinate progress, makes us fear the detour. But I take it anyway. Shaken but somehow also warmed by the idea that the GPS, at least, feels I have a life worth calculation.

Vagaries and Apostasies: A Litany

Let us begin:
Perhaps I'm too concerned with matters financial, about getting
another ride or two in before the end of the day, to make
enough for rent, for the car payment.
Perhaps it would be nice to know I'll have enough.
Perhaps the constant scramble for enough keeps me young.
Perhaps grey hair, like scars, adds character.
Perhaps I should get that tattoo, the prism, diffracting dark
light into rainbow; seems like a nice metaphor.
Perhaps she's out there, isolated, quarantined, half of a longed-
for whole.

Perhaps it's too late to save the planet.

Perhaps I've been wrong about everything. As in: Every. Single.
Thing.
Perhaps an orange comes with its own bag.
Perhaps I'm overthinking.
Perhaps the palpitations are not about stress.
Perhaps I should get that checked.
Perhaps it's best not to know.
Perhaps "coffee" was just coffee.
Perhaps it's not the planet that needs saving.
Perhaps none of this is real.
Perhaps idiosyncrasy is the ugly shirt you wear on casual
Fridays.
Perhaps I should get that tattoo, the gargoyle; seems like a nice
metaphor.
Perhaps this is the right path, though it looks overgrown with
wrong.
Perhaps I did it my way.
Perhaps I'm an idiot.
Perhaps the sides of the same coin have different values.
Perhaps a blind squirrel is content finding only the one nut.
Perhaps the reason you never see elephants in trees *isn't*
because they're so good at it.

Perhaps Dad jokes aren't funny.

Perhaps I should get both tattoos, since they are in many ways the same metaphor.

Perhaps fortune cookies are as good a guide as anything.

Perhaps apostasy is a question worded imprecisely.

Perhaps an outlier is merely the center of a circle that has yet to be drawn.

Perhaps destination is a glue-trap we just decided to decorate.

Perhaps I won't recognize it when I get there.

Perhaps I never left.

Perhaps I carry it with me.

Perhaps its unbearable lightness is the whisper of a choice I have yet to make, the import of which hardly matters.

Perhaps that's why this burdensome freedom is such delightful agony, because each stab of pain, each uncertain happenstance, announces that it is indelibly, gloriously, mine.

Fallow

In a new and strange countryside,
I see in an empty, harrowed field
a volleyball net. No ball,
no markings to define out of bounds,
nothing but the net
amongst the scattered detritus
of another's harvest.

Entertainment, perhaps,
for scarecrows after their
long season of vigilance?

Or have I reached a landscape
where games linger,
stubbornly insist upon
their right to be played?

A harmless, essential idyll,
while one waits for the time
to seed again, waits
for cultivation to resume.

Thanksgiving

"a river, suffering because reflections of clouds and trees are not clouds and trees."
Czeslaw Milosz

It's cool, skewing to coldish, this morning. And quiet. A rural quiet here in the heart of the city. In the park across the street, a few stubborn trees cling to threadbare leaves. Fall foliage muted, dull ochres and browns, a languid palette further dulled by the cold wet of mist. Fog masks buildings that pass for skyscrapers in this part of town, fifteen or twenty stories that qualify them for something—success, maybe, or just an elevated view gilded as success.

Here on the ground, you can see things well enough.

When you don't have a family, today is just a Thursday. Painted more dull and grey, perhaps, than all the others.

Somewhere, cousins and uncles spend the morning hunting, deer and elk. I have heard the bull elk bugle, but it does not bugle to me.

In its stead, I hear the cobwebbed silence of memory, that realm where fathers and mothers scowl from dreamscape Wanted posters, where sisters plan premature graves, where the shadow outline of sons dance to songs I no longer hear.

Tomorrow, those shadows will string up strands of colored lights, put up a fake tree, adorned with the ornaments of shared lives. There will be football on (although only one of them watches). A feast of Timon, the invitation lost within blue serge and gas lamp.

I think maybe I'll put up a strand of lights as well, tentacling up the handrail to the second story landing where I like to watch mornings (even—perhaps especially—quiet, misty ones). Since it's just a Thursday, maybe later I'll grade some papers, read a book, play some Xbox. Tradition demands I fix a meal, so I will. I think I'll cook up some andouille, perhaps with some crawfish tail. Cooked in butter and garlic. With some peppers and onions.

It's not the tradition, I know, but it will feed me. And isn't that what tradition is all about, anyway?

Slowburn

There is something about a fuse,
the slow burn of its inevitability,
its whisper of trajectory uncontained,
its hint of dazzling skybound pageantry,
and a looming brisance that threatens,
in its moment of fulfillment,
to put the stars to shame.

Buying Condoms at 51

It was so much easier when I was young. The last time I had to worry about condoms, there weren't so many options. "Ribbed, for her comfort" was about as exotic as they got. Now, they've got kinds with warming lubricants, kinds that desensitize (which, it turns out, is not meant ironically); you can get them ultra-thin, bare skin, or raw (which I did not chose, for it makes me think of sushi, the sting of wasabi). The reservoir tip has been labelled "classic," like Chuck Taylor's or cherry-limeades a callback to a quaint, long-ago era. Even the ribbed options have become more complicated. There are spiral ribbed, ultra-ribbed, and extra-studded. There are Nirvana packs, Ecstasy, Fire and Ice, and something called Ultra-Sensitive (which I probably should have picked, since I tend to cry afterwards). I even found a pack called "G-Spot Premium," which I hope comes with a map.

Before, one worried about size, made Magnum jokes, but now it's become a quantity issue. It is very difficult to find anything less than a sixty pack. The condom industry seems far more sanguine about my dating success than I do. What if I die with 57 still in the box (a number reached only because I made balloons out of two of them, because some things never stop being funny)? What will whoever finds the barely-used box think of me?

When I was young, I'd buy a box every two weeks simply to impress the pharmacist; now I bought a 36 pack (the smallest I could find) on Amazon because I was too embarrassed to approach the girl at Walmart and ask her to open the glass-display case. I did not subscribe to the Auto reorder program, though. There seems no need. This box should last until the end of my days, either because I am dead, have reached the age where only funny balloons suffice, or, I indeed "get lucky" (not 36 times, just the once) and reach that simple complicated destination, that return to the dream oasis, where nothing needs be purchased, because nothing is for sale.

Baggage

On this cool, wind-scoured final day of the year, I watch a
figure and his suitcase gimp across the faded-fawn park grass.
It's over 60 degrees, but he's huddled against the uncertainty of
future weather. Faded down jacket the color of static, what was
once a tattered scarf around the neck, the insistent defiance of a
cowboy hat.

Later tonight, better-dressed crowds will gather in warm rooms,
with their hors d'oeuvres and champagne and the paper-thin
security of trinkets, blithely unaware of the suffocating weight
of their collective errata.

This lurching man, prophet and prophecy, will not be among
them. Nor his suitcase, not dragged behind like he's a
misplaced traveler, but clutched to his chest like a prized
possession or a beloved child.

I do not know if this is his relocation or his disburdening, but
understand either is more instructive than the counting down
of minutes and seconds, or the hollow celebration of false
renewal and soon-to-be-broken resolutions.

Lights On in the Reptile House

In a small New Mexico zoo, my son stands before glass,
wonder-rapted, as the snake glides across and up the polished
surface. I watch him watching. I've been to enough
herpetariums to know such movement, such activity, is rare.
I'm sure he knows this as well, yet I understand that is not why
he watches with such reverence. I feel deeply that I am no
longer a part of that world; there is just the snake and just my
son. This erasure of me is prophetic, of course, but there is no
sadness; not yet. Just a surge of warmth. The kind you feel the
first time you ride a roller coaster, the first time you fall in love,
the first time you see a wild animal in its proper setting.

Because that's what's happening here. As my son watches the
snake and, perhaps, the snake watches him back, he
understands what he is looking at (as do I). There is no cage, no
recreated terrarium. There is just the snake and just my son.
There is no cage. As there was never meant to be. As, I hope, it
shall always remain.

Not the Poem It Was Meant to Be

In a long-ago writing workshop, I listened to a renowned fiction writer explain the concept of "definitive action"—an early gesture or act that immediately and fully conveys to a reader the character of a character. I understood what he meant in an academic way, like I understood Antarctica was cold, that Winona Ryder will not respond to my texts, that I would not enjoy eating porcupine.

This poem, however, was not supposed to be about "definitive action." This was supposed to be a love poem. Specifically, about love-at-first-sight. *More* specifically, about love-at-first-sight as it applies to the woman across the street, walking her dog in the park, as I watch from the window of my new apartment, steaming cup of morning coffee in my hand and the world refulgent with sun ray and possibility.

I have been working hard on listening to the Universe lately, and that decision has resulted in this wonderful new apartment and in a new sense of peace, the chasing away of what were daily heart palpitations, a reduction of the anxiety that had become a milieu. And now the Universe—the best dating app one could imagine—seemed speaking to me once again.

I have been told by a friend I have a type (although I married outside of it—and look how well *that* turned out) and if that is so, the woman with the dog without question fits, is perhaps more that type than Danielle, than Cassady, Storm, and the others (yes, you too, Winona). She is raven-haired, slender and lithe. Is wearing a T-shirt that seems (I resist—for the time being, at least—grabbing the binoculars for a better look) to promote an indie bookstore. The dog she is walking is a greyhound. A mere few hours ago, I was searching the Oklahoma chapter of Greyhound Rescue, idly pondering when the Universe would whisper about adopting a dog, finally filling that 17-year, ex-wife induced absence.

There was no need to wonder what the Universe was saying about this woman, though. I heard It loud and clear. And I felt the stirrings, saw the possibilities unfold, began trying out first lines. In short, I was ready to love again. And then, it happened: the dog arched its back, a canine question mark, and dropped, with paced intervals, deposits. When it was done, when it re-straightened its spine, the dog and the woman resumed their walk along the park pathway.

There was no bag, there was no clean-up. Just a deposit of dogshit left behind, as if it was someone else's problem. That, and nothing more; other than a poet, watching from a window across the street, shimmered in equal parts disappointment and disgust, but *listening*. Listening with a new, profound understanding of what "definitive action" means, alongside a healthy respect for the importance of revision.

An Itinerant Without an Itinerary

Morning Harvest

There's a sunrise to Oklahoma,
shades of pink and orange
that don't exist anywhere else.
Clouds non-committal
but honest; their integrity
a reminder that truth may not
always look the way we'd prefer it.

A ghostly harvest of fog and mist,
gilded in early
morning light wafts
from the fields straddling
the highway. I
make my way through
this early morning promise,
letting thoughts slide away, letting
urgencies melt, float along
with the morning vapors.

This cold January morn
a reminder that my world
is not the only one that matters, that
the puzzle piece is, after all, just a piece.

Important, yes, but one of countless many.
An assemblage, a portrait, that while it differs
from what came before, and will change again in
the looming soon, contains
the unfathomable beauty of Now.

The Measure of Distance

The lakes in Oklahoma are not interested in anything as cliché as clear blue water. Here, the lakes make the poet work, to find word and image to capture a watercolor that exists nowhere else, that is, in very real ways, unimaginable to the disembodied reader. Sometimes all the poet can do is dip his toes into this water, let it pet his feet with rhythm, as he soaks in the day's waning light, dusk's rays striking off layers of cloud in Neapolitan sunset, and think of other things:

That on the coast, the sunsets have both cloud and ocean to play with; that on the coast, the waves offer a broader embrace, packaged within an erasing susurrus; that an atlas ascribes a foolish significance to distance.

Sunsets—like distance—are an illusion, a fantastical sleight-of-hand, the sun disappearing only to come around behind you to light your way once again, as always.

The issue was never really in doubt. The measure of distance is meaningless. It is still water. These are still clouds. And this is just a moment.

Ugly Shirts and Chucks: A Self-Portrait

"It is time to explain myself"
Walt Whitman

They never seem very happy, those artists in their self-portraits. Van Gogh and the rest. Always frowning or scowling. Some have the vacant stare of trauma. It would be hard to imagine them wearing cargo shorts, or chewing bubble gum. It would be next to impossible to think of them roller-skating, bird watching, or telling a joke (except, perhaps, Dali, but then it would be a joke no one got, punchline and set up inextricably intertwined).

My father wore suits. Crisply-creased, pin-striped suits. Pressed and heavily-starched. Business casual was a polo shirt for the golf course, where he kept his membership to the last. I have no memory of him in shorts and he did not chew gum. He always wore suits. Pressed and heavily-starched. In *his* self-portrait (which he would pay someone else to do), he would not be scowling *or* frowning underneath his trimmed mustache (an ill-advised minus sign of hair). He would somehow manage to do both. Leaving me with only that other option.

So I wear ugly shirts and Chucks. A swirl of jellyfish or toucans or dinosaurs within which I hide; colorful footwear noticed only when one looks down.

Better Than Nothing

A post-work cold beer,
on the landing,
on a beautiful
mid-May Saturday,
with no one
to share the moment,

is not ideal, nor
particularly desirable,
laced as it is
with a faint taint
of melancholy.

But still:

It is a post-work cold beer,
on the landing,
on a beautiful
mid-May Saturday.

Christmas Morn

The silence this morning seems more profound than any other silence on any other morning. In the apartments around me, construction workers and retail clerks indulge in an extra hour of sleep. Children open the gifts they've inquisitively shaken for days. There is talk of Santa and the birth of a lord. It's been years since I've seen the inside of a church, have long since stopped believing in the stories they tell there. Still, I would be a fool not to catch the solemnity of this calm, silent morning.

But the birds flittering around me do not chirp, "Merry Christmas." Tardy stars do not gild this morning with anything other than their routine glory. Squirrels hoard nuts for themselves; they are not gift-givers. They do not have days like this in Nature, singled out and weighted with artificial significance. Despite what nativity sets would like to suggest, the ox and the ass do not care about our notions of a savior.

But despite this, despite my own stifled belief, I find, encased in this auroral silence, a desire to go along with it, to embrace the idea of a holy day. Even though my holy is not my neighbors' holy, nor the holy of children ripping into paper and foil, it shares a notion of harmony and goodwill. A certain kind of peace, and an opportunity. This hush of our own making subsumed into a larger, constant one that enfolds us all.

A Haiku That's Just Nuts

There are five (now six)
poems in this collection
that have squirrels in them.

Found

It's a matter of perspective, as most things are. We always consider the haystack from the searcher's point of view. We fail to understand the needle's agony of dread anticipation, of hearing, muted through dried and countless layers, the haphazard susurrus of parted fronds, of separated strands, or the gambol of searchers between the bales.

Fail to understand the needle's own hollow self-deception, lies about time and chance that echo in the carved-out chambers of its long-neglected heart. Or the wondrous strangeness of rediscovered purpose that follows the unaccountable moment of discovery, the delayed reward for the sustained darkness of alone.

The best part of being lost is its unwhispered correlative. A joy the insect trapped in amber, the mammoth frozen in polar ice awaiting the thaw, the other side of a coin hidden until the flip, can never know. The joy of the needle, freed from the haystack, polished by discovery, once again going about its blithe, natural task of making things whole.

In the News: For Dorothy Alexander

On the day we learned
of your death, I read in the news
a story about an underwater
volcano somewhere in the
South Pacific erupting,
the outflow of lava creating
a brand-new island.

A little piece of earth,
unsullied yet by the things
you fought against,
free still from the injustices
you made your cause.
This idea will, perhaps, give
a small comfort to those of us
who knew you,
those of us who will try
to follow where you've led.

It is the least the world can do,
gift us something new
on a day when it took so much.

Wonderful

My friend was telling me a story about a recent game of Scrabble when he mentioned one of the other players came up with a word he described as "wonderful." My friend could not recall the precise word. All he could offer was that "it was something like, 'bagel.'"

Bagel! That's the representative word he came up with. As an example of a "wonderful" word, Bagel.

My friend has three degrees related to the English language. He has been teaching English at the college level for over twenty years. One would have to assume the depth and breadth of his mastery of the language should allow him to pull up a more impressive word choice than "bagel."

And it's not like it's a particularly impressive word in the scheme of Scrabble scoring. It's only worth 9 points (yes, I looked it up). I've spelled "hirsute" and "tapenade" in a Scrabble game (yet somehow still lost). *Those* are "wonderful" words.

And this has *nothing* to do with any negative feelings toward the signified. I *love* bagels. They are a noble contribution to the breakfast lineup. But my friend did not grow up in the New York-New Jersey-Connecticut tri-state area, so his sense of "bagel" can only truly be called theoretical.

But now that a few days have passed, now that time has allowed my shock (laced with a tint of outrage, if I'm being honest) to subside, and I've had that time to think on this some more (a lot more, actually. I may need a hobby. Or a girlfriend), I must admit the following:

My friend is also a poet—a far better poet than I am, hiding behind the kitsch of the prose poem as I do. And as the Scrabble story shows, he understands something about words that I have yet to learn: they are a currency. While the snob or the neophyte may celebrate the hundred-dollar bill as innately better than the one-dollar, if you have a hundred singles, they buy the same thing, and buy it with a grace and style that the casual, flippant unrolling of a C-note can never approach.

My friend has incorporated, in the same way a leaf incorporates sunlight, a truth I have only gleaned. That if the poem is the outward expression of an inner world, if it is the song of a beautiful soul, as his poems are, then every word, no matter its Scrabble score, is wonderful.

Nevermore

I'm trying to write a poem, to no real avail, when the phone's ping gave me an excuse to pause in this desperate struggle, this vacuum of idea and word. It's a text from my friend. A recording of her partner, Jillian, impersonating a crow. It was really good. Shockingly so. If you close your eyes (and I did) you could believe that a crow was calling you on the phone. I listen to the clip several times (better than trying to write a stubborn and recalcitrant poem), and pondered the many questions provoked:

I ponder ability: how does one discover they can flawlessly impersonate a crow?
I challenge word choice: can one impersonate something not a person?
I contemplate loneliness: why don't crows call me on the phone anymore?
I question envy: why don't I have a partner who can imitate a crow? Or imitate a partner?

But then a crow—a real crow—caws from outside, and a thought more worrisome presents itself: what if I have it all wrong, and it wasn't Jillian imitating a crow, but crows imitating Jillian?

At the end of the clip, the crow-cawing stops, replaced by the very human giggling of my friends. That laughter pure frivolity, the poem I'd been seeking all morning.

The Fragility of Aphorism

While it was only a maxim, and like all maxims, fraught with arbitrary significance, it still caused quite a stir at that long-ago meeting, when the leopard padded in with incontrovertible proof that it could, in fact, change its spots. The impact was, without question, tremendous.

The gathering of dogs immediately set about learning new tricks. One of them, a Corgi named Bruce, became a world-renown billiards star, a fixture on late-night ESPN. Another, a Shar Pei named Rollo, is now a mainstay at the Bellagio, her long-running magic show hailed for never repeating itself.

An old longhorn successfully bought a gift to celebrate his friend Goat's marriage (his fifteenth), negotiating his way through fragile wares and aisles with a balleretic grace, nary a plate chipped or scratched.

An ostrich stared down looming calamity with forth-right honesty and self-critical integrity (although all the rats she knew abandoned her side. There were limits to the miracle, it must be admitted).

The birds learned that there were enough worms for all, the fish discovered, that with just a slight willingness to be uncomfortable and a positive outlook, they could function very well out of water, thank you very much, and camels' backs became as sturdy and reliable as a Ford (and with better gas mileage), no matter the straw.

From the moment of the leopard's entrance that day, all the crocodile's tears were sincere, clams felt free to discuss their depression, the owl failed Calculus (but, to be fair, who didn't?), and the elephant forgot why it was there.

We understood that sometimes the dead horse had it coming, and that it was haughty arrogance that in fact killed the cat.

From that day, we were no longer fettered by the pithy phrases of humanity, thoughtlessly thrown about when they were stymied for words, when their creativity abandoned them, when they found the appeal of hiding truth behind hollow phrases that rolled off the tongue like breath mints irresistible.

Yes, it was a great and glorious day, when the leopard showed up in stripes, and showed us how fragile were the things holding us back.

Roadkill

On a desolate stretch of Texas road, three black vultures perch on a forgotten billboard. The sign, floating above the stunted mesquite like a faded, regretted tattoo on the sky, reads, "Space Available."

Things must be bad in the Afterlife, if they need to advertise.

I hope they don't notice me; I'd rather not stop.

I'm making such good time.

Nesting Dolls

He left without saying good-bye, the boy who would run out to the playground, declaring to those in the house that he was off to make a new friend. And he usually did. In kindergarten, he told the class he wanted to be a zookeeper when he grew up and no one giggled, because that seemed right. He had a silly laugh, easily earned.

He left without saying good-bye, the man who took the woman he loved to a bonfire on their first date, inhaling woodsmoke along with her. She said something to him in French that he didn't understand. Soon, he gave up trying, because syntax was enough for now. He wanted to hold hands with her in the moonlight, but told her this too late. They married other people, because they were young and foolish. Despite this, he has an unshakable conviction that their meanderings will lead them back to each other one day, so he remembers his silly laugh, easily earned.

He left without saying good-bye, the lover who always had a lollipop working to keep his tongue in practice. In bed, he was like the host of a party, solicitous about his guests, with just the right amount of Falstaff in his revels. He understood touch the way a dove knows sky.

He left without saying good-bye, the father who would pull his awe-struck sons in turn across the ice, back-skating at speed that startled, enjoying the lactose burn in his calves. He would read them bedtime stories; Richard Scarry and Maurice Sendak. Occasionally mixing in Thoreau, just to see if they were paying attention. He made sure that their cake had extra frosting, that they received an extra serving of bubblegum.

Alone now, the man stares at himself shaving. His better years, he feels, are behind him. Old, overweight, balding, and poor, he's not quite the catch anymore. An off, off-Broadway show. So off Broadway, he's Ohio. He reads Tennyson's "Ulysses" and understands it now, viscerally. Sometimes he cuts himself on purpose, to watch the blood drip proof. He still has the silly laugh, easily earned. And upon occasion, it calls back the others, who peek from behind the man's reflection, their eyes a-twinkle with the mischief of memory, with the stubborn defiance of Ithacans, with thoughts on tomorrow, who never said good-bye, because they really never left.

Fortress of Solitude

The realization that you cannot
make one choose rightly, that
you can only be
the right choice,

brings with it
a profound peace.
It is a cold peace, with
only the glacier, and
the wind to give
it witness,

but it is a peace.
And it is profound.

Ode to that Old "Special" Sock

You were my partner in crime in those long-ago days of youth, a nylon and cotton evidence-hiding sleeve, the gathered, off-white stain-crunch of teenage release.

You were the surreptitious subversion during the last years of a dying marriage, when those normal marital outlets were no longer available.

But now, my long-time friend, now that I live alone and single, am free to spray wherever I want without the slightest compunction, the slightest fear of discovery or rebuke, you are once again just a sock, rolled up with a partner into a tight ball, banished to the darkness of a dresser drawer to await your bi-weekly summons, barrier between a weary and years-crinkled foot and a faded pair of Chuck Taylor's.

But we had a good run, and know that if the situation warrants, I shall call on you once again to take what my perpetually aroused, ever-youthful body has to give.

What It Feels Like

We have a penchant for martyrdom, at least, for someone
else's. We set up holidays and celebrate it. Christmas. Easter. If
the martyrdom is unpleasant, or does not fit into our
comfortable hermetics, we whitewash it, and celebrate anyway.
See: Thanksgiving.

And so, every February, we champion the champion of Love,
getting the story confused. From one way of looking at things,
Valentinus was nothing but an arrogant guest in Emperor
Claudius's house, insisting his host drop his own gods in favor
of another's. Most days I'm willing to forgive him his intolerant
proselytizing, his being consumed by a worldview to the
fanatical exclusion of all others. For that is what love feels like.

Before his death, Valentinus wrote *one* love letter. That's it! One
damn letter. And for that, Hallmark has re-crafted him in their
own image, the epitome of the Lover. And so, we exchange
gifts of flowers and chocolates. Valentinus is also the patron
saint of asthmatics, and of beekeepers, but just try giving your
true love an inhaler or some honey and see what happens. I
read somewhere that Claudius had Valentinus beaten, stoned,
and then beheaded. I believe this, for that is what love feels
like.

In 1929, Al Capone sent seven Valentine's, all to the same
address: 2122 North Clark St. Seven men jerk-danced to the
Thompson submachine jukebox, their bodies pockmarked by
.45 kisses. This is as it should be. Writhing and riddled. For that
is what love feels like.

This year, and the handful of years before and, one presumes,
the succession of years to follow, there is only self-love left for
me. The adolescent in us will smirk, misreading that term
(although, as I've made clear elsewhere, I'm not opposed to
that particular pleasure. I'm not dead yet, after all). But even
when I had someone to send things, I dismissed the holiday as

artificial, a codification of something meant to be habitual and organic.

But then again, all traditions are artificial. And when they wear out, or no longer fit just right, maybe we don't dismiss them, but alter the concepts to fit a changed world. So tonight, I will treat myself well. Let myself pick the movie, cook a carefully crafted meal, open a bottle of wine, let its evanescence blend into the atmosphere of apartment, and profess my profound affection for the fathomless silence within. For that is what love feels like.

On Landing

The first cool morning after
the infernal hell of an
Oklahoma summer.
The year's slow death
now believable.
Only crickets,
overnight-weary,
and the fledging light
for company.

I've traded in my balcony
for a second-story landing
fronting a new apartment,
that already feels as
comfortable as a favorite
sweater or a hound-dog's
welcoming nuzzle. It's a
smaller space, but it's
the vantage, not the space,
I often need.

A parade of feathers
Dopplers around the corner,
five ducks and two geese,
joined in formation, each making
their distinctive sounds,
taught to us long ago
on a See n' Say toy.

Beautifully disharmonic yet not
a cacophony, each call distinct,
yet also part of something new,
something never heard before and,
after they take one lap around the
dew-glimmered park across the street
and then fly back east into the

nascent, growing, light,
will never be heard again.

It's hard to think this jazz ballet
wasn't intentionally staged
just for me.
A welcome and a reminder both:
That wonder is always just
around a corner; that no matter
where one is in life, novelty can,
and frequently does, find you.

Of course, just as likely,
the birds did this for themselves.
Some blissful performance
of avian spontaneity,
done solely, unthinkingly,
for the pleasure of the moment.
A welcome and a reminder both.

Solitary Journey

"We live as a we dream—alone."
Joseph Conrad

Day 1: I-40

A light rain spits on the parched
earth. The horizon hidden beneath
overcast sky. The city is silent
this early hour. Only Scissortail Bridge
and its sequenced rainbow lighting
to wish me safe travels.

The local rock station is playing
AC/DC's "Ride On,"
as apt a soundtrack for this drive
as anything. Bon Scott's calm defiance
in the face of loneliness. There is a dead
dog on the side of the Interstate.
It has only one head instead of three.

Driving west, because that is our myth,
our Manifest Destiny. The trope of
riding off into the sunset. But do I
have to wait until the sunset to
chase the horizon? Or can I just assume,
based on habit, where it will be?

The sign for Fort Reno Visitor Center
strikes me as overly optimistic. So does the
"Joan Jett 4 President" spray-painted
on a barnside in Weatherford.

The Texas panhandle
seems unfinished; a place someone
meant to get around to, or back to,
and forgot; a scenic hiccup

between red earth and mesa.
The pushpin of Amarillo a sprawling
absurdity under an atmosphere of
fanaticism and cow shit.
Eat a 72-ounce steak in one hour—
the most American thing ever.

Driving down the Sandia,
there are two storm clouds saturating
the dry earth, spectral grey jellyfish
floating above the valley, returning water
from whence it came in the hope
that something grows.

New Mexico sky vast with shades
of blue cloud. Some say they hold
promise; some say they hold
nothing. I assume both are right,
and that it matters little.

Day 2: Albuquerque

When I was younger, I went to zoos
alone without concern, without
a second thought. Went to restaurants,
movie theaters, and water parks as well,

but I feel anomalous here, a bloody thumb
hitchhiking against the current, like
I've broken some social contract,
coming here without kids,
without a partner. I feel watched.
Side-eyed. An oddity. To some,
I am a threat. They grip their kids
tighter as I lean in to watch
hyena or capybara. I try
not blame them.

There is a polar bear I've been
coming to watch for years. His fur
has a mottled green skein to it,
the result of living too long
in an environment not his own.
I wish to set him free,
to let him wander, like I do now.

I exit earlier than
intended. I'll leave the zoo
to the kids, to the families, today.
There are other things to see.

Day 3: Carlsbad Caverns

There is something primal and
soothing about the familiarity
of a favorite place,
the air churned by cave swallows,
the pungency of their ammonia,
welcomes me again.

I've come here so many times
before. Pulled down by regret
and the echoes of those not with me,
I've returned, to be swallowed
by the great maw once more.
If there is such a thing as a salve
for the soul, I'll find it here.

In the realm of speleothem, a kindness
is offered. I am embraced by
a coolness that does not chill,
am offered a new perspective
on darkness. Ears ring
from the silence. A recalibration
is offered. The "what ifs," the "whys,"
the "should haves" fall away,

paltried by the rock surrounding.

In the Big Room, within reach of the handrailed
walkway, a stalagmite and a stalactite are separated
by a few fractions of an inch.
There will be a day, eons from now,
when they touch, and I,
and the things that trouble me,
will be long gone.

For the first time in a long while,
I feel re-situated. Later tonight,
I will return for the bat flight,
and I will not envy them their release,
their blithe freedom into an atmosphere
of their choosing.

I dismiss the elevator to the surface.
It only takes one up; it does not take one out.
Instead, I reverse the trail meant
to bring you down, hike back up
the 800-foot descent, ascend 80 stories,
emerging from this stone womb
with as much of the placidity I found within
as I can carry.

Day 4: Rt 82, Carlsbad to Alamogordo

The road west is so deserted here
the idea of lanes seems superfluous,
like the irrelevancy of choosing
which side of the bed when
it is just me.

Looking up into the endless
placid blue above, it's easy to believe
I'm driving on an ocean floor,

the one-time domain of
trilobite and plesiosaur.

I pause occasionally to binocular
pronghorn on the plain, this
lone vestige of the Paleocene,
mislabeled "antelope," unrelated
to anything other than itself,
at home on this scorching seafloor,
ocotillo and yucca replacing
coral bed long ago; gangly beasts
pulsing with suppressed speed,
perfectly suited to this barren and
broken land.

At Cloudcroft, elevation 8,650, I can see
the gypsum glimmer of White Sands
on the horizon, nestled
between two mountain ranges,
the horizon shimmered like a mirage.

A tunnel at the edge
of the Lincoln National Forest
births me back into the world.
A gorge on the right,
a scar of such great beauty,
demands I stop
and pay tribute.

A thunderstorm
gilds the gorge with light,
thunder reverberates against
its own echo.
Sitting on a wet boulder
at the chasm's edge,
watching the descending drops
below catch momentary sun,
I'm not being rained on so much

as rained through.

Other travelers are staying in their cars,
waiting out the storm before
continuing the descent into the
valley below. I've been driving through
storm clouds my whole life.
I'll drive into this one.

And the one after that.

Day 5: Emory Pass

Sunrise at White Sands,
toes buried under cool gypsum.
So quiet, I imagine I can hear
individual grains slide.
Can hear a lone beetle
scurry across what to him must be
incomprehensible vastness.
Until I came here, I did not understand silence.

Some friends worry about this trip,
about me. Because I tried once before,
they fear I came on this trip to die.
While I can't dismiss the possibility,
I have other motives.

If I *was* so inclined,
this would be a good place to do it.
Just wander off and let
the wind and undulating dunes
erase me. But there is still
so much to see.

The Very Large Array is closed
to the public today, so I adjust plans,
decide to take the Emory Pass

over the Black Range Mountains.
It is a dangerous road, I'm told.
Sheer drops, no guardrails,
Death always a few inches
away. When is it not?

The Pass is named after William Emory,
who led the Army of the West over
these mountains in1846 to "liberate"
California from the Spaniards. As if
that is how liberation is achieved.

At the top of the Pass,
before massive green folds
of some giant slumbering saurian,
before this second set of undulations,
ones that do not erase, but fill,
I stop for a simple lunch of
sliced tomato on bread,
a few pieces of bacon
held in reserve from breakfast.

A waterfalled creek trills behind me
as a mule deer watches, her gaze
bold and unafraid. She approves
my decision to take the Pass.
I feel sorry for William Emory.
I understand why he had to go, but
I cannot account for his leaving.

Day 6: Petrified Forest National Park

An itinerant without an itinerary,
I head further west, into the varihued
palette of the Arizona desert.
Although I'm alone, I say
the Dad joke aloud anyway:

"I don't know why these trees
are so scared."

It's a hollow joke, meant
to deflect. The truth is it
is not the trees that are scared.
I've been afraid most
of my life.

I was here before, thirty
years ago, but none of this
is familiar. I was too young, then,
to see; to listen.

I think Thoreau would have understood
these lands with an atavistic certainty.
Like him standing upon Katahdin,
I'm asking for "CONTACT," and
hiking down and around
Blue Mesa, I find it.

Strata upon strata of eons
whisper: "you will never have
enough money; you will never
have enough free time, so stop
waiting for that day. Do
the things you want to
do in the time you've been
given, while you have
the strength to do them."

They tell me the soul
must stretch its legs
more than once a year; that
the spirit cannot be caged by fear.
They speak of the difference
between sadness and sorrow,
tell me which one to keep,

and which to let go.

Day 7: Rt 550, San Juan Mountains

It is time to stop scurrying,
to stop chasing the horizon.
There is no need anymore.
The horizon is nothing but
a tomorrow luring us
with promises
it never intends to keep.

The kisses of the Arizona sun
still warm on my skin,
lingering remembrance
of a temporary but necessary
lover, I parabola back East.
A return cannot simply be a retracting;
that way is closed, now, so I head
up into Colorado to learn
what it has to teach.

I have not taken any pictures
on this journey. It is not that kind of trip.
Photos boil the essence of a moment
down to two dimensions. It is not memory I want,
but presence. Full, feeling presence.
The kind not found in the taking of pictures.

The problem with feeling, though,
is I hammer myself with it, over and again
beating myself up with regrets,
obsessing about the things I could have done
different, the things I should have improved.
Until it is impossible to think there is anything else.

I used to worry that whatever experience
I was having meant I was missing

countless other experiences. And of course,
that is true; it is just irrelevant.

Near Red Mountain Pass, the ascent impossibly continues,
until I'm convinced it can only end at cloudbank.
And yet, there are still mountains looming beyond.
Mountains as far as I can see.
It is impossible to think there is anything else.

From this height, everything else is left below.
From this height, the idea of forgiveness
is easy to believe in.
From this height, I understand
from where it must be offered.

Whatever mistakes I've made, whatever my share
in the sunderings of these years past,
I've paid that bill, over and again
and then some. It is time to start
celebrating the things I've earned,
the things I deserve.

I deserve to see the bald face of mountains,
tree-bearded, looming over these forests;
to see them reflected in the shimmering
lake at Molas Pass. I've earned this view
of the bighorn ram, as immobile in his defiance
as the rock upon which he stands.
I deserve to hear the scolding Steller's jay
accuse me of trespass; to see elk through
my sunroof sunning themselves on a saddle side.

One should not supplicate for happiness.
It is ours to breathe like mountain air.
I have paid my bill, and then some.
I refuse to live in the echo any longer.

Day 8: Continental Divide

For a long while, I thought it was
only a bad John Belushi movie. Only
later did I learn it was about choice,
and following the path available
to that choice. It comforts me
to know that even continents
have their crossroads.

I decide to cross at Independence Pass,
at 12, 095 feet, the highest paved road
in the country. So narrow it feels
like a game trail, and I am thankful
for the trees jammed against the edge.
They provide the illusion of containment,
prevent a full understanding of
the drop to the right.

I brought ghosts with me on this trip.
Those who have been taken from me,
those who walked away.
I've been carrying their luggage this whole time.
This seems like the right place to
put it down, leave them behind,
let them slide down the other side.
Unlike Orpheus or Lot's wife,
I've been allowed to look
back, without additional punishment
beyond this backward glance.

Half a mile from the summit,
I see movement. An elk feeds
not fifty yards from
the pullout. He is glorious.
14-point velvet-covered antlers
that seem too big for his head.
He glances over to confirm

I'm content with the distance,
am not one of those foolish people
destined for YouTube videos,
then resumes feeding,
deleafing a shrub.

It is so quiet, I can hear him chew.
As I think about leaving,
resuming this journey, he turns again,
full on, fixing me with a glare
profound and chiding,
one that speaks of the vast difference
between alone and solitary.

Coda:

The final hotel door closes.
I will be content to sleep
in my own bed tonight.
My mother told me long ago
to take everything I can
from a hotel room. To do
so now would seem like a desecration.
This journey is not about taking.

At a gas station along the road home,
an ephemera of bird-flock waft beneath
the paltry white of parking lot light
in search of a roost. I understand their need
but no longer share their quest.

It is true I never caught the horizon,
but that is because I was looking
for it in the wrong place.
It is not in the west; we carry it within us.

A Meal of the Moment, To Nourish the Now

Neologism

Sometimes the right word does not yet exist. So you have to make it up. An exercise of pure creation, a product of unfettered and defiant poetic will. A meal of the moment, to nourish the Now.

Words, like traditions, can calcify, fade into a hollow routine of shadowy import. But a body is a patchwork of scars; within, the soul draws a map outlining There to Here.

So, when an editor, or a proofreading friend points out that "remergent" is not a word, suggests that I mean "re-emergent," I must politely (for they have not traveled the road and always mean well) push back. "Re-emergent," insinuating, as it does, a second coming, will never fit. The caterpillar does not come from the egg and then the cocoon, genuflecting its way into repetition. One can't do something again that hasn't been done until this very moment, this specific, newly-nourished slice of Now.

And so, I "remerge." And most days I convince myself the word means something.

About the Author

Paul Juhasz was born in western New Jersey, grew up just outside New Haven, Connecticut, and has spent appreciable chunks of his life in the plains of central Illinois, in the upper hill country of Texas, and in the Lehigh Valley in Pennsylvania. Most recently seduced by the spirit of the red earth, he now lives in Oklahoma City. A graduate of the Red Earth M.F.A., his work has appeared in several literary journals, most recently *Concho River Review, Poetry Quarterly, Oklahoma Review,* and *Main Street Rag.* He has been serving as curator and coordinator of the Woody Guthrie Poets since 2020. His first book, *Fulfillment: Diary of a Warehouse Picker*—a mock journal covering his six-month stint in an Amazon warehouse—was published by Fine Dog Press in 2020. His second book, *Ronin,* a collection of (mostly) prose poems—also published by Fine Dog Press— was named a finalist for the 2022 Oklahoma Book Award in poetry. His second collection of poetry, *The Inner Life of Comics,* was published by Turning Plow Press in the fall of 2022. A collection of short fiction, *As If Place Matters,* was published by Fine Dog Press in the fall of 2023.

www.ingramcontent.com/pod-product-compliance
Lightning Source LLC
Chambersburg PA
CBHW020403130626
46549CB00006B/2412